5 ELEPHANTS

ROB LAIDLAW

Fitzhenry & Whiteside

Dedicated to elephant advocates everywhere and to the more than 1,000 park rangers who have been killed trying to protect elephants and other wild animals.

Published in Canada by Fitzhenry & Whiteside,
195 Allstate Parkway, Markham, ON L3R 4T8

Published in the United States by Fitzhenry & Whiteside,
311 Washington Street, Brighton, Massachusetts 02135

10 9 8 7 6 5 4 3 2 1

Fitzhenry & Whiteside acknowledges with thanks the Canada Council for the Arts, and the Ontario Arts Council for their support of our publishing program. We acknowledge the financial support of the Government of Canada through the Canada Book Fund (CBF) for our publishing activities.

Library and Archives Canada Cataloguing in Publication
5 Elephants
ISBN 978-1-55455-316-7 (Hardcover)
Data available on file

Publisher Cataloging-in-Publication Data (U.S.)
Laidlaw, Rob.
5 elephants / Rob Laidlaw.
[80] pages : col. photos. ; cm.

Summary: "With their huge size, giant ears, amazing trunk and incredible intelligence, elephants are unique in the natural world. They play a key role in the ecosystems they inhabit, but they're also highly individual, remarkable creature. Through the lives of five famous elephants, this book looks at fascinating elephant facts and figures and serious challenges that wild and captive elephants face." – Provided by publisher.
ISBN-13: 978-1-55455-316-7
1. Elephants – Juvenile literature. 2. Elephants – Biography – Juvenile literature. I. Title. II. Five elephants.
599.67092 dc23 QL737.P98.L 2014

Text and cover design by Tanya Montini

Front cover image (elephant) courtesy of Rob Laidlaw
Back cover image (elephant profile) courtesy of Jo-Anne McArthur/We Animals
Back flap image (author) courtesy of Zoocheck

Printed in China by Sheck Wah Tong Printing Press Ltd.

CONTENTS

INTRODUCTION

You might be wondering why this book is entitled *5 Elephants*. Like most books about elephants, this book is intended to provide you with some fascinating elephant facts and figures. I also want to tell you about some of the serious challenges that wild and captive elephants face. To truly understand elephants, though, we need to know more than just some basic information about how they function and live. We must also get to know them as individuals. We must learn their stories. That's why I've called this book *5 Elephants*. It features the stories of five famous elephants.

Two of those five elephants, Lucy and Tarra, are still alive today, and their stories continue to unfold. Tusko, Echo and Thandora, the three other elephants featured in this book, are no longer with us, but their stories and legacies live on. I hope you'll be inspired by all of them.

Elephants are truly remarkable, unmistakable animals. Their huge size, giant ears, amazing trunk and incredible intelligence make them unique in the natural world.

Everyone recognizes elephants. They've been featured in stories, cartoons and movies; they've appeared in circuses, travelling shows and zoos. The elephant is one of the world's most popular animals.

Throughout the years, I've visited some of the locations where wild elephants live, and I've been able to observe elephants in captivity all over the world. I've also been involved in many campaigns to help both captive and wild elephants. Through those campaigns, I've met many people who work tirelessly to help elephants. I call them the Elephant Guardians. They provide hope for elephants everywhere.

Elephants in captivity and in the wild are in trouble and need our help—now more than ever. So read on, learn and become inspired, so that you, too, can become an Elephant Guardian.

Calves are the most protected members of an elephant family. Echo had at least eight calves.

ONE ELEPHANT
THE NATURAL LIFE OF ECHO

The year was 1945, and World War II was coming to an end. In the shadow of Mount Kilimanjaro, Africa's highest peak, a female **elephant calf** was born. Her name was Echo.

Echo was tiny, weighing just a couple of hundred pounds. The ground vibrated as her mother and family members moved carefully around her. Echo made repeated attempts to stand for the first time. Finally, she stood up, although she teetered for a while. Her stance strengthened as the minutes went by. Her mother provided gentle support with her trunk and foot.

In just a couple of days, Echo would begin travelling. The **matriarch** of her family group would ensure everyone travelled at Echo's pace. For now, she was the most valuable part of the family; her family would do anything for her.

Echo was born in an area controlled by the Maasai, an African people famous as both warriors and cattle grazers. Despite living in a dry region, Echo and her family were able to spend a lot of time in lush swamps. The water came from the melting snow of the nearby mountain. Like any youngster, Echo loved to play in the water.

In the wet season, when food was plentiful, Echo and her family sometimes walked to other areas. To a young calf, these areas seemed far away. At times, the family would encounter other elephants on these journeys.

For the first few years of her life, Echo sought comfort and safety from her mother and family members. Whenever she was startled or frightened, she'd run back to her mom and receive a reassuring trunk touch or rub. Protected by her family, she was safe from most of the natural hazards that might threaten her. As part of a family, Echo gradually learned all the lessons she'd need to survive later in life. As she grew into her teenage years, Echo became a key member of the family, and at the young age of 23, she became the family's matriarch, the leader of the herd.

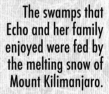

The swamps that Echo and her family enjoyed were fed by the melting snow of Mount Kilimanjaro.

In 1972, scientist Cynthia Moss began the Amboseli Elephant Research Project. She attached radio-collars onto several adult elephants to track their movements. One of them was Echo. The elephants' activities throughout the years would be recorded by photographer and filmmaker Martyn Colbeck. The Project would become the longest running elephant field study ever conducted.

Cynthia chose to track a family with two adult females, two adolescents and three **calves**. They were known as the EB family. In the EB family, all of the elephants were given names starting with E; that's how Echo was named.

Shortly after the study began, part of Echo's home range officially became Amboseli National Park. The park was small, at just 392 square kilometres (150 square miles). Sometimes Echo and her family would travel beyond its boundaries, but Echo understood that the park was a safe haven her family could always return to.

During her life, Echo mothered eight calves: Erin, Eamon, Enid, Eliot, Ely, Emily Kate, Ebony and Esprit. In 1982, Erin gave birth to her

With the help of family members, Echo rescued her daughter Ebony after she was kidnapped by another elephant family.

Echo the matriarch is one of the most studied elephants in the world.

own calf, Edwin, which made Echo a grandmother. The family was slowly getting larger.

In 1985, Echo's son Eamon mysteriously vanished. No one knows what happened to him, but many people believe that the Maasai might have killed him. That same year, Echo gave birth to a new calf named Eliot. There were many happy moments, but there were some challenges, too.

When Emily, the second-oldest female elephant, died, Echo and the EB family were deeply affected. Emily had been eating trash from an unfenced garbage pit, and the trash had damaged her insides. After Emily's death, her six-month-old son, Edo, got thin and weak quickly. He needed his mother's milk, but it was gone. Edo was caught by wildlife officials and taken to an elephant orphanage to recover.

In 1990, Echo gave birth to Ely. However, Ely was born with bent legs that made walking difficult. Echo was a patient and caring mother, though. The other family members would travel to find food and water while Echo stayed with her baby. At first, Ely could only shuffle along on his knees while Echo moved slowly alongside him. After three days, Ely's feet and legs loosened up and he was able to walk normally. During this difficult time, Echo showed a great deal of determination, devotion and love for Ely.

In 1994, Echo's eighth calf, Ebony, was born. In a show of dominance, another elephant family kidnapped Ebony. Echo was a protective mother, though, and she and her family confronted the captors and brought Ebony back to the herd.

Throughout the years, Echo led her family through both hard times and times of plenty. The family would forage in the swamp, graze in the pastures, rest in the scrubland, socialize with each other and meet up with other elephant families.

Tragedy struck suddenly when Echo's daughter Erin was speared in the side. The wound became infected and, soon, Erin was unable to walk or even suckle her baby properly. Echo stayed close to her daughter, but the situation worsened. It was clear that Erin was not going to recover. There was nothing that Echo could do. She approached Erin, touched her trunk, and then left with her grandchild. The family would visit Erin's carcass and bones later on.

Echo's life had been long and full. She had led her family through happy times and harsh times. But old age and tough conditions caught up to her. She was 65 years old when she collapsed and passed away.

So much of what we know about the lives and relationships of elephants has come from studying Echo, the EB family and the other Amboseli elephants. They have provided us with a glimpse into the complex lives of elephants and forever changed the way we think about these astonishing animals.

Echo's life was rich and meaningful and her legacy lives on.

Tiny calf Ely shuffles along on bent legs while Echo and Enid stand guard.

Echo's family members had rich lives with lots of difficult challenges and many happy times.

CHAPTER 2

THE ELE-FACTS

WHAT'S AN ELEPHANT?

Elephants are the largest and heaviest living land animals. They are **herbivores** that have **lifespans** similar to humans. Echo's group lived on the savanna, but elephants can inhabit a broad range of environments, from hot, sandy deserts to lush, tropical forests. They can live near ocean coastlines or high up the sides of mountains. Elephants are **keystone species**, one of those animal species that serve a unique and critical role in the **ecology** of the wild spaces where they live.

ELEPHANT ANCESTORS

Elephants are part of the *Elephantidae* family, which is part of the larger zoological order *Proboscidea*, meaning animals with trunks.

As elephants evolved, they spread across the world's continents, except for South America, Australia and Antarctica.

One of the most famous elephant relatives is the now-extinct mammoth. It was a large, hairy member of the *Elephantidae* family. The mammoth's long hair, layer of blubber and other adaptations helped it survive throughout the north, although many mammoths also lived in southern areas as well.

The last surviving mammoths are thought to have lived on Wrangel Island in Russia until they disappeared around 1650 BC. One of the earliest members of *Proboscidea*, however, is the extinct *Stegodon*. It is believed that *Stegodons* gave rise to modern elephants.

The last surviving mammoth was still alive when the Great Pyramids of Egypt were constructed.

MODERN ELEPHANTS

Today, three elephant species exist: the African savanna (bush) elephant (*Loxodonta africana*), the African forest elephant (*Loxodonta cyclotis*) and the Asian elephant (*Elephas maximus*). The African elephants appeared 4 to 6 million years ago, while modern Asian elephants likely surfaced between 2 and 4 million years ago.

There are three different subspecies of Asian elephants: Indian, Sri Lankan and Sumatran. Some scientists believe the pygmy elephants on the island of Borneo are a separate Asian species, while other experts argue that some other populations of elephants are also distinct species. Until recently, experts believed the African forest elephant and African savanna elephant were the same species, but DNA testing proved otherwise.

Elephants only have a few living relatives left. These relatives are hyraxes, which are small furry mammals that look like rodents, and manatees and dugongs, which look like walruses without tusks.

The relatives of modern elephants don't look anything like elephants.

This map shows the areas where Asian elephants live today.

WHERE ARE WILD ELEPHANTS FOUND?

The two species of African elephants used to be found everywhere in Africa south of the Sahara Desert, in areas where there was sufficient water and food. African savanna elephants inhabited the savanna zones, while African forest elephants lived in the dense jungles of west and central Africa. However, due to elephant **poaching** and an expanding human population, elephant ranges have been greatly reduced. Today, African elephants can be found in 37 countries, many of them in relatively small, fragmented habitats.

In the past, Asian elephants were found from Iraq, across Southeast Asia, and into southern China. They are now mostly confined to hilly and mountainous regions in parts of India and Southeast Asia, including the islands of Sumatra and Borneo, where forests still exist and human contact is minimal. Unfortunately, many Asian elephants live in habitats that are too small to sustain them in the future.

ELEPHANT HABITATS

In areas where there is sufficient food, water, shelter and protection from humans, elephant home ranges can be as small as 14 square kilometres (5.4 square miles), but in other areas, such as dry savanna, an elephant's home range can be larger than 11,000 square kilometres (4,247 square miles). Within their home ranges, elephants move about, often walking substantial distances every day. They travel through rich, varied terrain, which may include hills, grasslands, rainforests, swamps, deserts and mountains. In the wild, they experience a diversity of natural sights, sounds, smells and textures every day.

Wild elephants live in a wide variety of environments, including deep forests and jungles.

HOW MANY ELEPHANTS?

There aren't as many wild elephants today as there were in the past. In 1979, approximately 1.3 million elephants lived in Africa, but in 1989—just ten years later—that number dropped to just over 600,000. Today, there are approximately 400,000 elephants left in all of Africa. More than half of all African elephants are gone, due to poaching. In some regions, herds have been reduced by 80% or more, and in other areas, they have completely disappeared.

Asian elephants are forest dwellers, so estimating their total population is difficult. We believe, however, that there are approximately 35,000–40,000 Asian elephants left, with almost half of them living in India. While we don't know their previous numbers, experts are sure today's population is only a tiny fraction of the number there used to be.

The massive size of adult elephants protects them from most predators.

3

ASTOUNDING ADAPTATIONS

BIGGER THAN BIG

Stand beside an elephant and one thing is clear—elephants are big. There are many advantages to being large, but there are also some drawbacks. One advantage is protection. Few predators are capable of taking down an adult elephant. A small number of African lion prides have been known to hunt juvenile and adult elephants, but it is a risky endeavor. Elephants usually just chase the lions away.

Being as big as an elephant has another advantage: it usually guarantees a spot in a preferred feeding area, water hole or salt lick. Other animals will move aside and wait their turn. Size can also help in accessing food and water. An elephant can get at food that is high in the trees and in spots that are out of reach to most other animals. During dry times, they can even dig with their tusks and feet and create their own water holes.

Of course, being big also means you have to eat a lot, so elephants spend a great deal of time foraging for food. Elephants can't digest cellulose, a significant compound in plants, so a lot of what they eat passes right through them. That's why wild adult elephants eat 100–200 kilograms (220–440 pounds) of food every day.

For some elephants, like those that live in the rainforest, food may be plentiful and easy to find. For others, such as the Namibian desert elephants, food and water can be scarce and hard to locate. It is hard to imagine that a desert could support an elephant population.

The largest species is the African savanna elephant, also called the bush elephant, with the biggest bulls reaching a shoulder height of 4 metres (13 feet) and a massive weight of more than 6,000 kilograms (13,000 pounds). That's more than the combined weight of 75 adult men. African forest elephants are not quite as big and have smaller ears.

The largest Asian elephant bulls, on the other hand, can stand 3.2 metres (10.5 feet) tall at the shoulders and reach a

An elephant trunk is a nose, hand and water siphon all in one.

An elephant's trunk is strong, flexible and sensitive. It is unique in the animal world.

weight of 5,400 kilograms (11,900 pounds). Asian elephants have smaller ears, and their highest point is at the middle of their backs, not their shoulders like the two African species.

PACHYDERM PROBOSCIS

The elephant has many features that are unique in the animal world, but few are as recognizable as its trunk. Gradually over millions of years, the elephant's nose and upper lip fused together and extended to eventually become the trunk.

While some people think the trunk is just a long nose, because running along the interior of the trunk are an elephant's nostrils, it's also an elephant's "hand." Since it contains no bones, the trunk is flexible and can move, curl and bend in any direction. The trunk contains an astounding 60,000 muscles, which means it's strong, too.

It can also be delicately manoeuvered. At the end of the trunk are triangular "fingers," two for African elephants and one for Asian elephants. By using these fingers, an elephant can pick up tiny objects, like a single coin off a tile floor.

The trunk has another important function as well. When an elephant wants a drink, it siphons water into the trunk and then sprays the water into its mouth.

TITANIC TEETH

Elephants have unique teeth. For most of their lives, elephants have just four teeth at a time: one upper tooth and one lower tooth on each side of their mouths. They don't have any teeth in the middle.

Elephant teeth have ridges that are used to grind food. As an elephant grows, the old teeth are worn down and slowly move forward to make way for a new set of teeth. The remnants of the old teeth eventually just fall out. An elephant will have six sets of teeth during its lifetime.

Each tooth of an adult elephant is the size of a brick and can weigh up to 5 kilograms (11 pounds).

Tusks are also considered to be teeth. These start out as little "milk teeth" in infant elephants, but they are replaced during the first year of life by real tusks. Tusks grow continuously throughout the elephant's life. Since elephants use their tusks for tasks, such as digging, uprooting vegetation, ripping bark or moving objects, the tusks can wear down or sometimes even break off. A broken tusk will continue to grow, although at a slower rate. Some elephants have tusks that have grown to be several metres long. Female Asian elephants are usually tuskless, but they do have **incisor teeth**, called **tushes**, which grow slowly and often can't be seen because they don't protrude out far enough.

Some elephants have tushes, which are small tusks that don't protrude far out from the face.

THOSE FEET ARE MADE FOR WALKING

Having the right kind of feet is especially important if you're the heaviest land animal on the planet. Elephant feet are large and oval-shaped, and the leg and foot look a lot like a tree trunk. You might expect elephants to be clumsy when they move around, but they are not. They can easily walk on many different kinds of terrain. They have even been known to walk along narrow ledges on the sides of mountains and find their way along jumbled, rocky paths in the total darkness of caves.

If you looked at an x-ray of an elephant's lower leg and foot, you'd see something quite surprising. While their feet appear rather stumpy, elephants actually walk on their tiptoes. Behind the toes, a mass of soft tissue called a **digital pad** acts as a shock absorber. The pad helps distribute the elephant's weight and cushions each step. It also allows elephants to walk quietly. To gain traction, the soles of their feet have small bumps, ridges and cracks. Elephant feet must be sturdy and strong for walking long distances every day, an activity that keeps them healthy and fit.

An elephant's foot is made for walking long distances over a variety of terrain.

AIR-CONDITIONING EARS

African elephants have large ears that are shaped similarly to the African continent, while Asian elephants have smaller, floppier ears. Elephants often have difficulty cooling off, so they take mud baths, go swimming or stand in shady spots. They also flap their ears to move air over their bodies, like a fan. The flapping is also a built-in cooling system. Warm

Even though it looks tough, elephant skin is surprisingly sensitive.

blood from the body circulates up through the ears, where the flapping cools it down, before it is sent from the ears back to the body. The hotter the weather, the faster the ears flap. Ears are critical for keeping cool.

SENSITIVE SKIN

An elephant's skin looks tough. In some areas, the skin can be up to 1 inch (2.5 centimetres) thick. Elephant skin can also be thin in certain areas, such as behind the ears, around the mouth and on the inside of the legs near the belly. What's really surprising is how sensitive elephant skin is. Elephants can feel a gentle touch of a finger. In the wild, elephants will often cover themselves with dirt or take mud baths to protect their skin from the sun or biting insects. Elephant skin isn't as tough as it looks.

ELEPHANTS WILL OFTEN COVER THEMSELVES WITH DIRT OR TAKE MUD BATHS TO PROTECT THEIR SKIN FROM THE SUN OR BITING INSECTS.

Playing is a regular part of a baby elephant's daily life.

CHAPTER 4

ELEPHANT LIFE

WILD ELEPHANT DAILY LIFE

At first glance, it might seem like elephants live simple lives, just standing around or slowly foraging for food. Nothing could be further from the truth. An elephant's daily life is actually far more active and complex than most people believe. In addition to the time they spend foraging or grazing, elephants also roam and explore, socialize with family members, meet up with other related elephant families, play, swim, wallow in the mud and perform many other types of activities. They'll rest, especially during the hottest times of the day, and sleep for a few hours at night, but most of the time, they're awake and active.

A FAMILY LIFE

The elephant is one of the world's most social animals. Females live in the same family group throughout their entire lives. Each family group is made up of a matriarch, usually the oldest, most experienced female, along with her sisters and daughters and their offspring. Echo and her family are a good example of a family group. The family members follow the matriarch's direction and leadership and depend on her wisdom and experience to ensure they are able to survive and be safe.

Elephant societies are exceptionally complex. Families often get together to form **bond groups** consisting of dozens of elephants, many of them related to each other. They usually forage and travel together, although some adult family members may travel on their own occasionally and then join up with the others later. Calves stay close to their mothers during the first few years of life and will suckle until they reach the age of 5 or 6. The young learn from their elders, and the **cow elephants** learn how to be responsible mothers. Females often help new mothers look after their babies. They will even babysit. These females are called **allomothers**.

The herd also provides protection from danger. If a threat is present, such as a passing pride of lions, the adults form a circle to protect the babies, which hide safely in the middle.

For many years, elephant calves remain under the watchful eye of their mothers and family members.

An elephant **clan** is an even larger social group made up of numerous bond groups. A clan can consist of a hundred or more elephants that get together occasionally, usually at times when food is abundant.

The **bull elephants**, on the other hand, leave the family group to live in bachelor herds when they reach their early teens, although some individual bulls may stay with their families until they reach 18 years of age. Once they reach sexual maturity, they'll be chased away from the herd by their mothers and other family members. Eventually they'll find and mate with the cows, but when the calves are born 22 months later, the bull elephants won't help raise them. Instead, they'll be back out on their own.

SMARTER THAN SMART

Elephants are huge animals, so it makes sense that their brains would be big, too. Their brains usually weigh between 4 and 6 kilograms (8.8–13 pounds). Elephant brains are also highly evolved, sharing some of the same characteristics as dolphins, great apes and humans.

When you look at how elephants live, it's clear they have to be smart. Adult elephants, particularly the matriarchs, are like computer banks of knowledge. They know the best routes to travel, where water can be found, the best feeding locations and the geographic features of their home ranges, which can be thousands of kilometres in size. They also retain a lot of knowledge about their family members and even other elephants. If they become separated for many years, elephants can still remember each other. The old saying that an elephant never forgets may actually be true.

Elephants also seem to understand and even mourn death. There have been many accounts of elephants visiting or encountering elephant bones. They'll stop, sometimes for hours, and take turns touching, lifting or sometimes even covering the bones.

Elephants can also solve complex problems. Videos on YouTube show female elephants figuring out how to get their babies unstuck from mud beds, wells or water-filled holes. Some elephants even invent and use tools. For example, elephants have been seen using

Elephants may stand by the body of a dead relative or visit the elephant's bones and spend time touching or even burying them.

branches to demolish electric fences, so that they can get to the other side without receiving a shock.

The incredible intelligence of elephants is a major reason why they need to live in complex environments, with lots to do and other elephants to socialize with. If they don't have those things, they'll quickly get bored and frustrated.

ELEPHANT TALK

Elephants in a family or herd keep in touch with each other almost constantly. They communicate through touches, body postures, chemical signals, scents and all kind of sounds, from squeaks and squeals to low rumbles and the distinctive loud trumpets. They can convey a lot of information in many different ways. They might be telling other elephants how they are feeling, whether they are ready to breed or, in the case of the males, to stay away because they're angry.

Elephants communicate in a variety of ways, including infrasound, which are low sounds that humans can't hear.

eLePHants can Detect THe GrounD vIBratIons THrouGH THe skIn on THeIr feet or THrouGH THeIr trunks.

Elephants also produce low rumbles called **infrasound**, which can travel long distances. Although humans can't hear these rumbles, we can sometimes feel them. Infrasound can travel 16 kilometres (9.9 miles) through the air or travel up to 30 kilometres (18.6 miles) through the ground. Elephants can detect the ground vibrations through the skin on their feet or through their trunks. So, even if an elephant appears to be all alone, it might be talking to other elephants that are far away.

Lucy's indoor space is relatively small and not very interesting.

TWO ELEPHANTS
CANADA'S LAST NORTHERN ELEPHANT

She was standing in the elephant house, leaning against the wall with her trunk hanging limp, the last metre of it coiled on the concrete floor. Occasionally, Lucy would shuffle to the barn door and look outside. It was cold, the temperature was below zero, and there was snow on the ground. She would stand there looking outside, rocking back and forth.

Lucy was born in the tropical wilderness of Sri Lanka. At 39 years old, she isn't considered elderly yet, but she is closing in on her early 40s, a time when many elephants in zoos die.

If Lucy were still part of a wild elephant family, she might already be a respected elder, helping to guide, teach and protect her younger family members. She would travel, forage, socialize and grow old with her family.

But Lucy is far from Sri Lanka. She lives alone at the Valley Zoo in Edmonton, a small northern Canadian city with bitterly cold winters.

Lucy spends a lot of time in the elephant house during the cold weather, shuffling around her small indoor space. She also has access to a yard outside, and a small, separate indoor exercise area. Weather permitting, the zoo staff takes her for walks around the property, sometimes in the snow.

Lucy is one of the most famous and controversial elephants in North America. Many people, including some of the world's leading elephant experts, want Lucy moved elsewhere. They hope that Lucy will one day get to live in a facility with more space, a better climate and, most of all, other elephants.

The story of how Lucy came to Edmonton, Alberta, began many years ago, in 1975, when the City of Edmonton decided to expand its Storyland Valley Zoo, a small children's zoo that featured displays with storybook themes, like the *Three Little Pigs* and *Mother Goose*.

The new zoo would be larger, more than 24 hectares (60 acres) in size, and would include an African exhibit featuring zebras, ostriches and other animals. The biggest attraction was going to be an elephant. At that time, every zoo wanted elephants, which were relatively easy to acquire.

In the 1970s, zookeepers could order baby elephants from animal dealers, so that's what the Valley Zoo did. The purchase was funded by a $40,000 contribution from Edmonton businessman S.C. Alldritt. From this donation, $10,000 was used to purchase the baby, while the remainder was used to construct the elephant enclosure.

With funding and plans in place, the Valley Zoo placed an order for a baby Asian elephant from a West German animal dealer. In a letter to the dealer, the Valley Zoo manager said he wanted "a healthy, evenly coloured specimen of approximately two years of age." The manager

In the 1970s, many zoos ordered baby elephants for their collections.

also mentioned that he would prefer a baby that was no longer drinking its mother's milk, but said they would accept "a milk-feeding animal if necessary." The zoo paid $8,939 for Lucy.

At the time, Lucy was named Skanik. The records are not entirely clear about where in Sri Lanka she came from, but some records indicate she was born in the wild. Some people claim she was an orphan. If Lucy was removed from her family in the wild, her mother would have done everything possible to prevent her from being taken. Her mother would never willingly give her up, even if it meant that she would also be captured or even killed.

ELE-CONSERVATION? Wild elephants have no problem breeding on their own. When they are protected from humans, elephants thrive, and their numbers increase. The major threats to wild elephant populations are illegal poaching for **ivory**, the breakup of elephant habitats and human-elephant conflicts. Keeping and breeding elephants in zoos doesn't address any of those issues and just leads to more captive elephants that will never see the wild.

According to the animal dealer, Lucy came with a whole group of animals that arrived in a shipment from India, making it impossible to trace her background.

In 1977, Lucy was put in a crate and flown to Alberta, Canada, from West Germany. Lucy had no idea what was going on. Her senses must have been overloaded with unfamiliar, terrifying new sights, sounds, smells and vibrations. She didn't know where her mother, aunts or sisters were. She would have called out, cried and whimpered, hoping to be rescued by her family, to stand protected by their bodies and to feel the gentle touch of her mother's trunk.

When Lucy finally arrived, she was greeted by prominent Edmonton residents and media. Confused and alone, all Lucy could

Samantha, an African elephant, lived at the Valley Zoo for almost 20 years.

do was wait to see what happened next. For the next 10 years—a time when Lucy should have been with her mother, family and other elephants—she lived alone at the zoo.

In 1986 and 1987, Lucy was sent to the Calgary Zoo, a three-hour drive to the south, for **breeding loans**. She was bred many times, but she never produced a baby. The breeding loans stopped and Lucy was alone again, at least for a while.

A couple of years later, Samantha, a baby African elephant that had been captured in Zimbabwe, was transferred to the Valley Zoo. Samantha was much younger than Lucy. She was also a different elephant species with different habits and ways of communicating. However, Lucy was no longer alone. She finally had company.

Like many zoo elephants, Lucy started to experience health problems. She had foot troubles, discharge from her trunk, arthritis, and bed sores on her face and hip. At times, she was also overweight, which would worsen the other problems as well.

Lucy gets a foot trim to prevent more foot troubles.

Lucy and Samantha's conditions were not optimal, so the City of Edmonton allocated $2 million to upgrade the facility. However, the new exhibit still didn't provide Lucy and Samantha with room to roam, hills to climb, pasture to graze, trees to pull down or places to swim. What's more, they were still stuck inside during the cold Edmonton winters, where the temperature can drop far below zero.

Lucy and Samantha lived together for years, but in 2007, Samantha was sent to the US on a breeding loan. She has yet to return. Lucy has been alone since Samantha left.

During her time at the Valley Zoo, Lucy has attracted attention. For many years, Edmonton residents, animal-welfare groups and people across Canada have been expressing concern about Lucy being alone in a cold climate. Thousands of letters have been sent to the City of Edmonton and the Valley Zoo asking them to send Lucy somewhere else. There have even been court cases. But the city and the zoo haven't changed their position yet.

The pressure of so many people speaking up for Lucy has caused the Valley Zoo to make some changes to the way Lucy is kept, including putting up an exercise structure for the winter. But she is still alone in a small zoo enclosure in a cold climate. They haven't changed that.

A wild female elephant spends her entire life in the same family. Females in captivity should always have the company of other elephants.

Some people say Lucy is an anti-social elephant, but leading elephant scientists say there is no such thing. Every female elephant should be in a family or in the company of other elephants.

Lucy won't be replaced when she dies, but the city and the zoo are reluctant to let her go. They claim moving her would be dangerous, possibly even life-threatening,

Top: Elephants live healthier lives in warmer climates.

Bottom: Concerned citizens and animal-welfare groups have been protesting to get Lucy moved to a sanctuary.

because of a respiratory medical condition that the zoo has had difficulty diagnosing. However, the zoo has also refused offers by Zoocheck and other animal-welfare groups to bring in a new independent team of expert veterinarians to help assess her condition.

Lucy was denied the opportunity to live a rich, natural life like Echo and many other wild elephants. Her life would be much better if she were allowed to live the remainder of it in the company of other elephants in a warmer climate. There might be a small risk in moving Lucy, but the benefit to her would make it all worthwhile.

I think if we could ask Lucy what she wants, she would respond by asking us, "When do we leave?"

Lucy is unaware that she has attracted so much attention and generated so much discussion. Let's hope it leads to a better life for Lucy and all other elephants in captivity.

In India and other parts of Asia, elephants are used in religious festivals and parades.

THE CHALLENGES OF CAPTIVITY

Both African elephants, like Echo, and Asian elephants, like Lucy, have been kept in captivity for thousands of years. Today, approximately 15,000 elephants are kept captive in zoos, circuses, travelling shows, reserves, temples and timber camps. India is the country with the most captive elephants—an estimated 4,000. In the United States, close to 300 elephants live in zoos that are members of the Association of Zoos and Aquariums, with a slightly smaller number being held in other zoos, circuses, sanctuaries and by private owners.

Like other animals held in captivity, elephants require food, water, shelter and veterinary care, but elephants have other important needs that often seem to be overlooked, ignored or dismissed. The Five Freedoms of Animal Welfare, a set of animal-welfare criteria developed in the United Kingdom in 1965, helps highlight what elephants need:

1. Freedom from thirst, hunger and malnutrition

2. Freedom from discomfort

3. Freedom from pain, injury and disease

4. Freedom to express normal behaviour

5. Freedom from fear and distress

To satisfy the Five Freedoms, captive elephants must have an acceptable climate, room to roam, complex environments where they can explore and forage, free association with other elephants and stable family relationships. They also cannot be chained or beaten. However, for many captive elephants around the world, the Five Freedoms are not satisfied. Even in many of the new modern elephant exhibits in zoos, which often cost millions of dollars, the needs of elephants seem to be overlooked. The exhibits are still far too small and barren.

Many new elephant exhibits look better, but they still do not satisfy the Five Freedoms of Animal Welfare.

ELE-FRIENDLY WEATHER

Modern elephants have evolved to live in tropical regions. While elephants can tolerate cool temperatures for short periods of time, there is a limit to what their bodies can handle. Cold climates with long winters may force elephants indoors, which can contribute to poor physical fitness, foot disease, bone problems, psychological problems and other issues.

ROOM TO ROAM

Elephants are extremely active animals. In the wild, they will walk, explore, forage, socialize, bathe and engage in a broad range of other activities for up to 20 hours a day. Depending on where they live and what season it is, elephants may travel anywhere from a few kilometres

IS IT REALLY ENOUGH? Wild elephants can range over hundreds or thousands of square miles of terrain during their lifetimes. The Association of Zoos and Aquariums (AZA) sets the minimum outdoor-space requirement for an adult elephant at only 500 square metres (5,400 square feet). That size is the equivalent of 33 parking-lot spaces—not much space if you're an elephant.

to tens of kilometres every day. To behave naturally, elephants require a lot of space, preferably tens or hundreds of acres, which they rarely get in captivity.

SOFT SURFACES, COMFORTABLE FEET

Elephants need to walk and exercise their feet on natural ground. They're not structured to stand on hard surfaces all the time. In the wild, elephants walk at different speeds and push, pull, stomp, rub and dig with their feet. These activities keep their feet healthy, moist, lubricated and in good shape. In captivity, elephants often stand around on concrete floors, or on hard, compacted soil, which can be a major factor in foot and bone problems. Foot problems are one of the biggest killers of elephants in zoos. All elephants should live on natural surfaces in order to maintain healthy feet.

For elephants in captivity, foot disease can be painful and even deadly.

EXERCISE AND ACTIVITY

To keep mentally and physically healthy, elephants need to stay active and engaged. Obesity among zoo elephants is a serious problem. A recent study of elephants in North American zoos revealed that many are overweight, with 40% being placed in the "most overweight" category. The key reasons for elephant obesity include consuming too many calories and not getting enough exercise. Being severely

Obesity in captive elephants can be caused by too much high-calorie food and not enough exercise.

overweight can decrease **fertility**, contribute to disease, such as heart disease, and can make arthritis, foot problems and skeletal conditions worse. Active elephants are healthier and happier.

Today, many zoos use **enrichment** to enhance elephant enclosures and increase elephant activity. Enrichment is a process in which zookeepers provide toys, objects, foods, activities and experiences to try to keep captive animals occupied. However, elephants need a lot of physical and mental stimulation. The best enrichment for elephants is a lot of complex, natural space, including pasture and woods, so they can roam, forage and explore and have other elephants to socialize with. They should also be kept in an elephant-friendly climate that lets them be outside most of the time.

If elephant spaces are too small, it may not matter what toys and activities are provided. The elephants will quickly get bored of them and they won't get enough exercise.

FAMILY AND FRIENDS

Female elephants live in the same family group their entire lives. The families will often have up to a dozen members of varying ages, and they all move, forage and socialize together, day and night.

Enrichment can be useful, but it isn't enough.

eLePHaNTS NeeD a LOT OF PHYSICaL aND MeNTaL STIMULaTION.

In captivity, unrelated elephants are often kept together, so they should be given an opportunity to establish their own bonds and friendships with other elephants. Zoo associations now recommend that a minimum of three elephants be kept together, but larger numbers are better. Some zoos still keep elephants alone.

Zoos often move elephants from one zoo to another, like when Lucy and Samantha were sent to zoos on breeding loans, but these moves are unnatural and the elephants have no choice. In the wild, female elephants live in stable family groups, often for their entire lives. Unlike the bull elephants, female elephants don't leave their families. In some captive facilities, elephant calves may be removed from their mothers—a separation that would never happen in the wild. No elephant mother would ever want to be separated from her baby. Removing babies or juvenile elephants from their families at any time, for any reason, should not be allowed.

STRANGE CAPTIVE BEHAVIOURS Many elephants in captivity act out some weird behaviours. They may repeatedly shift forward and backward, rock from side to side, bob their heads up and down, or stand completely still. Many of these behaviours are called stereotypies—meaningless repetitive movements. These strange movements don't occur in wild elephants and they indicate that there is a problem with the animal's living conditions. Sometimes, captive elephant mothers will reject their babies. This is an abnormal behaviour that doesn't happen in the wild. It might occur because of the stress of captivity or it could be that the new moms have never had older females to teach them how to take care of babies.

Since the 18th century, elephants like Tusko have been featured in circuses and travelling shows throughout the United States.

CHAPTER 7

THREE ELEPHANTS
TUSKO'S TOUGH TIMES

It was 1898 when he emerged from the bowels of the ship. He was confused. Just weeks before, he had been in the hot climate and forests of Siam, in the country that is now called Thailand. At just 6 years old, he was still a kid and he looked like one. Just 1.5 metres (5 feet) high, he was small and not particularly impressive. When his crate was lifted from the ship's deck onto the pier, he was officially in the City of New York. Little did he know that he would become one of the most famous elephants in the world.

Not long after his arrival, he was sold to the Lee Clark Wagon Show, which travelled and performed across the United States. He was given the name Ned and he was one of the show's four elephants. After finishing in one town, the show would pack up and move on to the next town. It was always the same routine. It was drastically different from the life Ned remembered back home in Siam.

As the years went by, Ned grew tall and large. Like all other male elephants, he started to experience **musth** during his adolescence. During musth, Ned would feel aggressive and, at times, he would challenge his handlers. He was just acting like all bull elephants do during musth, but he was labelled dangerous and difficult to handle. Whenever Ned came into musth, he was sent to the show's winter quarters in Texas. He was severely confined, but it was being separated from the other elephants that was most confusing and traumatic to him.

The show wasn't bringing in much money, so owner Lee Clark arranged a now famous stunt. Ned would battle some fighting cattle bulls in a ring in Juarez, Mexico, for $2,500. Ned easily knocked the cattle bulls down and won the fight. Later that night, he was led back across the border into the US. It was an unusual event, but Ned's life would become even stranger and his fame would grow.

In 1921, the Al G. Barnes Circus purchased Ned and renamed him Tusko. Along with several other elephants, he was a major circus attraction. Circus life is tough for elephants, and that may be why Tusko decided to go on a rampage in the town of Sedro-Woolley, Washington.

Just prior to show time, Tusko tossed his handler aside, injuring him in the process. Tusko then took off. The horrible leg chains Tusko was normally secured with had been temporarily removed so his handler could clean him off.

Captive bull elephants in musth are often kept away from other elephants.

MUST THERE BE MUSTH? When bull elephants mature, they periodically go through musth, a natural process in which the level of reproductive hormones rises. During this time, the bulls want to breed, and they can become unusually aggressive and violent toward humans and, occasionally, other elephants. During musth, temporin, a thick liquid, can often be seen running down the side of an elephant's head. Musth can last for a few weeks to a few months. During musth, bull elephants are often aggressive and, in captivity, they have to be kept separated from other elephants for their safety. For these reasons, many zoo keepers refuse to keep male elephants.

ES SUDDENLY

Children Mourn Great Elephant

Here is Tusko, the largest elephant in captivity in the world, who died this morning at Woodland park. Tusko is shown here surrounded by admiring Seattle children, hundreds of whom visited him daily.

DEEP MYSTERY IN DEATH OF GREAT BEAST

Huge Elephant Puts Up Valiant Fight, but Foe Too Strong

Tusko the mighty is dead. The largest elephant in captivity died at 7:55 this morning under mysterious circumstances at the Woodland park zoo, according to a bulletin issued by Dr. Gus Knudson, zoo supervisor.

The story of Tusko's last fight was a dramatic one. Dr. Knudson told of it. Knudson said he does not know what killed Tusko.

"The first we knew that Tusko was ailing was Thursday," he said. "He seemed to be weak in his hind legs. Yesterday afternoon he grew weak and lay down on his side, while exercising in the yard back of his house. Again about 10 o'clock last night he lay down in his house and we realized that he was seriously sick. I stayed with him throut the night—fighting to save his life. I gave him the medicine I thought would help him.

"Tusko was gone to the last. He struggled to get to his feet about midnight, when his temperature was rising to 103.

"He had to lie down again, but at 3 o'clock he made the last effort to get back on his feet as tho he wanted to stand up and fight. He collapsed and did not get up again."

Hundreds of boys and girls raced thru Woodland park this morning and, not knowing that Tusko was dead, clustered around the windows of the elephant house. "We want Tusko," they shouted.

The canvas blinds were tightly drawn over the windows and they could not see in to view the tragedy.

Knudson said that an autopsy may be performed in an effort to determine what caused Tusko's death.

Tusko, it is believed, was about 43 or 44 years of age. He was brought to this country many years ago, and was purchased from a wagon show by Al G. Barnes, the circus king. For years Tusko led the grand march in the circus until he ran amok in Sedro-Woolley in 1922. The last 10 years he has spent in chains, changing owners many times—the appetite of the great beast being too great for anyone to make a profit by exhibiting him.

During the past two years he has been in the northwest, and has been on exhibit in Woodland park since August.

His trainer, "Slim" Lewis, who has been Tusko's keeper for nearly 10 years, was broken hearted today. To him Tusko was not the dangerous animal, who had to be kept in heavy chains, but just a friend.

Tusko's 1922 rampage in Sedro-Woolley, Washington, made him one of the most famous elephants in North America.

Trainer George "Slim" Lewis spent more time with Tusko than anyone else.

While he was free, Tusko overturned cars, uprooted fences, damaged buildings and panicked a lot of people. He was trying to escape, but he didn't know where to go. Hundreds of men and boys followed him that night. The next morning, Tusko was cornered between two railway boxcars after having travelled a total of 48 kilometres (30 miles). He was tired and scared. His freedom was over.

After his rampage, Tusko was deemed dangerous, so he was pulled from the show and sent to circus headquarters where he stayed for two long years. During his periods of musth, he was kept in a crib so small he couldn't even turn around. More than anything else, Tusko wanted to be able to act like an elephant—to walk, forage and communicate with other elephants—but he was denied that opportunity.

While the real Tusko was gone, another elephant named Black Diamond travelled with the circus under the name of Tusko. Most people didn't know the difference. When the real Tusko returned to the circus, he was covered with chains, including **hobbles** on his legs, chains holding his tusks in place and a series of interconnected chains limiting the movement of his head and trunk. The rubbing of the chains led to skin sores that were difficult to treat.

Tusko was also expensive to feed, so the circus sold him to Al Painter, a showman from Lotus Isle Amusement Park in Portland, Oregon. Tusko didn't stay there for long, though, because just a year later, he was taken by yet another showman to the Oregon State Fair in the town of Salem. That showman had money trouble, so he took off and left Tusko stranded in Salem.

Since the town of Salem and the state did not want the responsibility of caring for a dangerous adult elephant, Bayard "Sleepy" Gray, one of Tusko's handlers who stayed in Salem, acquired ownership of him for next to nothing. George "Slim" Lewis, an elephant man who would end up spending many years with Tusko, soon joined him. Gray moved Tusko to the City of Portland to a small building—which was really more of a shed—that Gray was renting for $20 a month. Tusko was chained by all four feet and people could pay a dime to see him.

Tusko was considered dangerous so he spent much of his time in chains.

Tusko was frustrated. He wasn't able to move or exercise. On Christmas Eve, he managed to free himself from two of his leg chains and began demolishing the building's walls. The police were called. They were instructed to shoot Tusko if he broke free.

Although still chained by his rear feet, Tusko demolished one side of the building. He was able to step outside and feel some fresh air and a breeze. Large crowds of people had gathered and they cheered for him. The incident generated a high public profile. As a result, over 50,000 people came to see Tusko, but only after he was re-chained to the floor.

Tusko was confined indoors with chains on his legs for several months. He pulled at them to free himself but was not successful. The chains became painfully embedded in his legs. They were eventually cut off and his wounds healed. But Tusko still wasn't any better off because the old chains were immediately replaced with new chains covered with rubber.

Eventually, fewer and fewer people came to see Tusko. Public interest had dwindled, which meant fewer paying customers, so Tusko was moved to Woodland and then Chehalis, Washington, where he was kept in a large barn. A month later, Tusko was moved yet again

Tusko leads a procession of elephants in a 1922 circus parade through Sedro-Woolley, Washington.

and ended up in Tacoma. However, town officials didn't want a dangerous elephant, so they forced Tusko to leave. He had nowhere to go.

When news circulated that Tusko needed a place to stay, another showman named Bill Meyers offered to let Tusko stay on his expansive property.

For the first time as an adult elephant, Tusko was able to walk freely and graze in fields. He felt fresh air, sunshine, and soft ground under his feet. He foraged on tall grass and bushes. A short time after arriving, though, Tusko decided to walk away on his own, so Bill Meyers evicted him.

Chained to an open trailer, Tusko was taken to Seattle to be exhibited at Fleet Week, a celebration for marines and other navy personnel. On the way, the trailer tilted over and fell during a turn, leaving Tusko on his side with his feet still chained to the trailer. He wasn't hurt, so he was unfastened, the trailer was uprighted and the journey continued.

At Fleet Week, customers flocked to see Tusko in his tent. The money was good. A large sign was erected:

SEE TUSKO, TUSKO THE TERRIBLE, THE WORLD'S LARGEST ELEPHANT. HE STANDS 14 FEET TALL AND WEIGHS 11 TONS.

Those measurements were an exaggeration. No one knew if Tusko was the biggest elephant. As an adult, he stood 3.1 metres (10 feet, 2 inches) high and weighed about 6.3 tonnes (7 tons).

In order to draw a crowd, circuses and shows at that time often claimed that their elephants were the biggest or most impressive.

Tusko spent a few months in Seattle. He was in an unheated tent, chained in one spot. He was not allowed to go out for exercise. At times, Tusko was given toys, but they didn't keep him occupied.

Eventually, a meeting with Seattle's mayor, the local zoo, and the humane society took place. They decided that Tusko should be declared a public nuisance and moved to the Woodland Park Zoo. The zoo would hire his handler, George Lewis, to look after him. The zoo would become Tusko's permanent home.

Tusko was still in a tent because his enclosure was being prepared. At least his new home was heated, but Tusko still had to be chained all the time because the building's walls weren't strong enough to contain him. He now had an outside yard, but when he went outdoors, he was still wearing chains.

At the zoo, Tusko met Wide Awake, the zoo's other elephant. It had been a long time since Tusko had an elephant friend and he was very happy about it.

On June 9, 1933, George Lewis put Tusko and Wide Awake in their night quarters. When he returned for his 9 pm check, he saw that Tusko wasn't feeling well. Tusko sat back and couldn't stand up. At approximately 9:30 am the next morning, Tusko finally lay down on his side and passed away, possibly from a blood clot in his heart.

Tusko couldn't forage in the forest, swim in a river, or socialize with family or friends like a normal bull elephant. When he died on June 10, 1933, Tusko was 42 years old.

At the Woodland Park Zoo in Seattle, Tusko made friends with another elephant named Wide Awake, shown here.

In some parts of the world, elephants are a common sight on city streets.

CHAPTER 8

USING ELEPHANTS

For as long as they have coexisted, humans have been using elephants for their own personal gain. In the earliest days, elephants and their relatives were targeted by small groups of hunters as a source of food. Since the hunters were armed with only simple weapons, hunting an animal as large and dangerous as an elephant would have been a difficult task. Even so, many experts believe that the mammoths, mastodons and many other large creatures of the past were wiped out by early human hunters as people spread across the world.

Humans have also hunted elephants for their ivory. They've also used elephants as beasts of burden, war machines, religious symbols, entertainers, tourist attractions and hunting trophies.

BEASTS OF BURDEN

Anyone travelling to an Asian country, like India, Thailand or Myanmar, has a good chance of coming across elephants being used for work, particularly for **timber operations**. Elephants have been

used by the timber industry for hundreds of years; they are known as beasts of burden. An elephant's huge size and strength allows it to push down trees, or roll, push or pick up large logs. A bull elephant with large tusks can insert its tusks under a log, balance it correctly so it doesn't slide off, and lift it up like a forklift would.

Logging operations are often located deep within dense jungles, surrounded by uneven terrain and a lack of roads. When trucks and machinery cannot be used in these operations, elephants become particularly useful. There are still hundreds of elephants being used in timber camps in Asia. Elephant numbers are slowly decreasing as forests are being destroyed. Many out-of-work timber elephants are sold, donated to temples or even abandoned by their owners and left to survive on their own in the jungle.

WAR MACHINES

When elephants are used to help humans during times of war, they are known as war machines. The first known case of elephants being used as war machines occurred in Asia. With armour plates protecting

Elephants have been used in timber operations for thousands of years, but logging machinery and forest destruction are reducing their numbers.

their bodies and spears attached to their tusks as weapons, the elephants were sent into battle. Soldiers mounted on their backs carried weapons, such as lances or spears, to use against enemy soldiers on the ground.

After Alexander the Great encountered elephants in a battle with Indian King Porus, he acquired his own elephants and their use as war machines became more popular. At first, war-machine elephants came from Asia, but, later, African elephants were also used in battle.

In more recent times, elephants have been used as war machines, too, although not in battle. In modern wars, like World War II and the Vietnam War, elephants were used as beasts of burden or used to patrol the jungles, moving easily through areas that no car or jeep could access.

GODS IN CHAINS

In some cultures, elephants are respected, admired creatures that are considered almost supernatural in nature. In Hinduism, the God Ganesha has the head of an elephant, and in Buddhism, white elephants, which can be albino or just pale-skinned, are considered a living form of the Buddha. Today, hundreds of temples keep elephants. The elephants are dressed up, covered with decorations or painted a variety of colours for parades and special religious events.

Decorated temple elephants are routinely featured in Indian festivals and parades.

Keeping elephants in temples is a controversial topic in India and other Asian countries, as many of the elephants receive poor housing and terrible care. In May 2013, an Indian newspaper reported that 269 temple elephants, most of them under 40 years old, had died in the previous three years.

EARLY ELE-TAINMENT

In Asia, the Middle East and Europe, elephants have been featured in cultural and entertainment events for thousands of years. In some cases, the elephants were not mistreated, while other events were brutal and cruel to elephants.

Elephants have been used as performers for thousands of years and are still used in circuses and travelling shows today.

The first modern elephant to live in North America was an infant Asian elephant who arrived in 1796 on a trading ship. The ship's captain had purchased the female baby for $200 in Thailand and when he arrived in America, he sold her for $10,000. She was exhibited up and down the eastern coast of North America. The first elephant to perform tricks arrived in the early 19th century and survived for more than 20 years. Since that time, hundreds of elephants have been brought to North America.

MANAGING ELEPHANTS IN CAPTIVITY

Elephants held in captivity are usually managed by one of the three kinds of management systems.

 Free Contact (FC): When Free Contact management is used, keepers or handlers actually enter the elephant enclosure and interact directly with them. Many zoos, circuses and temples practice FC. This system usually requires establishing dominance over the elephants and can often involve the use of chains and a sharp tool known as the **ankus** to control the animal. Free Contact is the most controversial captive-elephant management system.

Protected Contact (PC): When Protected Contact is used, keepers only interact with elephants through specially designed barriers that make it safe to do so. Many zoos and sanctuaries now use this system.

 No Contact (NC): When No Contact management is used, there is no direct contact between keepers and elephants. Some of the large fenced game reserves practise this kind of management. Unless the elephants escape the reserve or are sick or injured and need medical care, they are left on their own.

In Protected Contact management, keepers only interact with elephants through heavy, elephant-proof barriers.

This old-style ankus is still used throughout Asia.

THE PAIN OF THE CHAIN

Chaining elephants is a routine practice in circuses and many zoos. It usually involves securing a chain to one front leg and the opposite rear leg. Elephants may be chained when they are not on display or not performing. Investigations have revealed that many circus elephants are chained from 12 to 23 hours each day.

Many working elephants in Asia may also be chained. Some street elephants have chains secured to their legs with the opposite ends attached to a tree or rock to prevent them from wandering off at night or when they are not working. Sometimes a hobble, which binds the legs together, will also be used. Chaining is an old practice that still occurs today because it's a cheap and easy way to restrain an elephant.

Being confined in trailers or rail cars is a regular part of life for many circus elephants.

Many elephant advocates call the ankus a weapon and would like to see it banned completely.

TOOL OF THE TRADE

The ankus, also called the bullhook or elephant stick, is a wooden, metal or fiberglass stick with a metal hook and pointed tip at one end. Handlers and trainers who work directly with elephants use the ankus to control and manipulate them. They apply the hook to a sensitive part of the elephant's body to cause discomfort or pain. The elephants don't like it, so they move away from the pain in the direction the trainer wants.

Unfortunately, elephant handlers sometimes use the ankus as a weapon to strike or poke elephants, too. Elephant Guardians are trying to ban the use of the ankus in elephant management.

LIFE ON THE ROAD

Just like Tusko did in the old days, elephants that perform in circuses and travelling shows today travel from one town to another, usually by truck or rail car. While travelling, the elephants are confined in small spaces. The cramped conditions prevent movement and rocking that might cause a trailer to overturn. It's not fun to be confined, so elephants shouldn't be spending a lot of time in travel containers. However, some travelling elephants are confined in rail cars for an average of 20 hours between towns, while others are kept in railway box cars for as much as 90 to 100 hours at a time.

Daily life on the road is also repetitive. Meals, exercise, play time and interactions between elephants are strictly controlled.

BEHIND THE ELECTRIC FENCE

Some circus and travelling-show owners erect electric-fence compounds when they are not on the move from town to town. These compounds can be set up in a parking lot, on an arena floor or outside in a grass or dirt area. While these enclosures allow more movement than chains, the elephants are usually only able to stand around or shuffle a short distance in one direction or another.

THE PLIGHT OF TRAVEL-BEGGING ELEPHANTS

Travel-begging elephants are owned by **mahouts**, traditional Indian elephant keepers or drivers, who depend on the income generated by these elephants to feed themselves and their families.

Many travel-begging elephants live in cities without permanent shelters where they are required to walk on hard, and often hot, pavement or concrete. They may be fed leftover restaurant scraps or food scavenged from dumps, in addition to whatever the mahout can afford to buy. Travel-begging elephants are often either overweight from eating bad food or extremely thin from not being given enough food.

GOOD NEWS FOR ELEPHANTS
ELEPHANT EXPORT STOPPED

When news got out that Zimbabwe was going to export two wild baby elephants to a North Korean zoo, thousands of people wrote to the Prime Minister of Zimbabwe urging him to cancel the sale. Renowned elephant expert Dr. Joyce Poole wrote one of the letters, which was signed by more than 50 organizations. The campaign was successful and Zimbabwe cancelled the sale. The two elephant calves were to be introduced to a herd of rescued elephants and eventually released back into the wild. Unfortunately, Zimbabwe later sent wild elephants to zoos in China. Stopping the export to North Korea was great news and other exports of elephants have been stopped as well, but, as the export to China shows, there is still much work to be done.

Travel-begging elephants are used for tourist rides and photos.

49

Expanding human populations reduce space and food for wild elephants and can lead to human-elephant conflict situations.

CHAPTER 9

HUMANS AND WILD ELEPHANTS

ELEPHANTS NEED HOMES

African and Asian elephants live in many areas with the world's fastest growing human populations. They often compete for space or resources with humans. There is also intense pressure, such as logging, road building and new human settlements, on the ecosystems that elephants need to survive. While there are still expansive elephant habitats in some countries, many elephants live in areas that are small, **fragmented** and unable to sustain them.

LET'S ALL GET ALONG

Each year, the number of human-elephant conflicts rises. Conflicts are often the result of human development intruding on elephant habitat. Sometimes normal elephant food sources are destroyed or blocked off by buildings, farms, fences, roads or railway lines, so the elephants have no choice but to venture into farmers' crops to find food. But farmers don't want elephants raiding their crops, so they often stand guard and make noise to scare them off. In recent years, other methods have also been tried. Solar-powered electric fences that give a shock when touched have been installed to keep elephants from wandering outside of parks and reserves. While they are not foolproof, electric fences are considered one of the most effective elephant barriers.

One of the most threatened elephant populations lives on the Indonesian island of Sumatra. Even though they are already near **extinction**, the elephants' forest homes are currently being converted into palm-oil plantations. Their traditional food sources are being destroyed. It is no surprise that the elephants have resorted to raiding farm crops.

These conflicts are not just risky to elephants. In India, hundreds of humans are killed every year by elephants. In June 2013, a herd of 16 elephants strayed into villages near Bangalore. Four people were killed. After the deadly conflict, officials herded the elephants away from the city, back toward Bannerghatta National Park.

The beehive fence is an inexpensive but effective way to prevent elephants from raiding farmers' crops.

GOOD NEWS FOR ELEPHANTS
ELEPHANTS AND BEES DON'T MIX

When wild elephants damage or eat farmers' crops, people get angry. To help minimize the problem of crop-raiding elephants in Africa, Dr. Lucy King invented a beehive fence. Elephants don't want to feed on trees where beehives are present because they don't want to get stung. So, Dr. King applied that knowledge to solving human-elephant conflicts. The fence consists of beehives, made of plywood with a metal roof, suspended by wires between wooden posts. If an elephant pushes on the fence or the wire, the beehive swings around, agitating the bees who come out to protect the hive. It's a simple idea that has been tested in several locations in Kenya. In each case, the beehives have greatly reduced the number of times elephants have crossed the fence.

Tusks grow slowly, but continuously, during an elephant's life.

10

LOOKING FOR GOLDEN TEETH

Imagine your teeth being more valuable than gold. An elephant's ivory tusks, which are really just elongated teeth made of a material called **dentine**, have been called "white gold."

Ivory has been a valuable, highly sought-after substance for thousands of years. It's been used for carvings, jewelry, knife holders, fans, billiard balls, piano keys and furniture. Although some ivory has been obtained from elephants that have died of natural causes, or even from uncovered mammoth remains, most ivory is taken from elephants who are killed specifically so their teeth can be removed. The **ivory trade** has resulted in millions of elephants being killed. It is one of the key causes of elephant decline in the world. Animal lovers and **conservationists** are concerned about the fate of elephants and have been working to stop the ivory trade.

Since ivory is so valuable and the demand is so high, the poaching of African elephants has dramatically increased in recent years. Asian elephants are also poached for ivory, which has become a serious threat to many populations.

TACKLING THE TOOTH TRADE

In 1989, at the meeting of the **Convention on International Trade in Endangered Species**, the trade in African elephant ivory was banned. Since that time, though, some countries were given permission to sell off old stockpiles of ivory, which created a way for new, illegal ivory to be **smuggled** into the system. Illegal ivory is also still being sold and traded on the **black market**. In fact, every time the international community has allowed old stockpiled ivory to be sold, poaching has increased.

Dealing with the illegal ivory trade is challenging, though. Some of the trade is conducted by highly organized criminals, known as the ivory syndicates, who are involved in poaching, international smuggling and selling of illegal ivory. In some areas, poaching is even conducted by private armies or **militias** that sell the ivory to fund their war efforts. Sadly, many brave people trying to defend the elephants have been killed by ivory poachers.

OTHER IVORY Other animals that produce ivory tusks are hippos, walruses, narwhals and even some pigs. However, none of them produce as much ivory as elephants, nor is their ivory as high in quality.

GOOD NEWS FOR ELEPHANTS
14-YEAR-OLD FIGHTS THE IVORY TRADE ONE SCHOOL AT A TIME

In October 2011, 14-year-old Celia Ho read the article "Blood Ivory" in National Geographic magazine. She was deeply affected by what she learned about the plight of wild elephants. She decided to write a letter to the South China Morning Post, her local Hong Kong newspaper. Her letter was published and noticed by Eco-Sys Action, a non-profit organization that fights for the protection of threatened species, like elephants. Soon, a partnership developed between Celia and the group, and Celia started a campaign to educate people about the ivory trade. Celia's slogan is "Schools United for Elephants." Her major targets are schools in China, and she hopes that each school she reaches will encourage other schools to get involved in the fight against ivory.

Countries around the world have burned or crushed their ivory stockpiles in the fight against poaching.

DESTROYING DENTINE

On July 19, 1989, the president of Kenya ignited a 10.8-tonne (12 ton) mound of ivory. Flames reached skyward and clouds of black smoke billowed as the ivory burned. It was a dramatic scene featured in news reports around the world. The event symbolized Kenya's commitment to stopping the illegal ivory trade. It was also meant to be a call for others around the world to join them in their fight. Two years later, Kenya burned a 6.1-tonne (6.8-ton) pile of ivory. Zambia burned its own ivory in 1992.

With an increase in poaching these past few years, Kenya wanted to draw attention to the plight of elephants once again, so in July 2011, officials burned another pile of ivory. And then the Philippines made a statement against the ivory trade by crushing their own ivory stockpile. Other countries have joined in by destroying their ivory as well.

GOOD NEWS FOR ELEPHANTS
JIM NYAMU'S "IVORY BELONGS TO ELEPHANTS" WALK

Jim Nyamu knew that Kenya's elephants were in trouble—they were being slaughtered by illegal ivory poachers. He also knew that his fellow Kenyans wanted the elephants to survive as much as he did, but some of them didn't know just how serious the situation was. But what could he do?

As the director of the Elephant Neighbor's Center, an organization dedicated to helping humans and elephants live in peaceful co-existence, Jim decided he would walk from Mombasa to Nairobi, a distance of more than 1,000 kilometres (621 miles). He hoped the walk would alert people in Kenya and around the world to the plight of the elephants.

On the morning of February 9, 2013, Jim began the first phase of his walk. In the sweltering heat, Jim set off with a small support team. He had no idea if anyone would really pay attention.

As the walk progressed, it became clear that people were interested. Newspaper, radio and television reporters came out to interview Jim about the walk and the plight of the elephants. As the news spread, people started to join in, including members of animal-welfare groups and students from the University of Nairobi and Kenyatta University wildlife clubs. Even the president's wife, First Lady Margaret Kenyatta, joined in for a segment of the walk.

With a large crowd in tow, Jim finished the first phase of the walk on February 23. The second phase of the walk took him from Masai Mara to Mount Kenya, more than double the distance of the first phase, a total of 2,210 kilometres (1,500 miles).

All along the route, Jim Nyamu spoke to schools, conservation centres and communities. He spread the word about the importance of elephant and wildlife conservation. He helped generate a renewed national interest and more than 10,000 signatures in support of elephant protection.

Carol Buckley looked after Fluffie at the tire dealership and later changed Fluffie's name to Tarra.

FOUR ELEPHANTS
TARRA'S JOURNEY TO SANCTUARY

She was just a baby when she was separated from her family and captured in the Burmese wilderness (Burma is now called Myanmar). She was then sold to an animal dealer. She had no idea how strange her life would soon become. It began with a long journey by airplane from Thailand to the United States in 1974.

After arriving in America, it didn't take long before a businessman named Bob Nance in Simi Valley, California, bought the baby elephant. She had wiry hair covering her body, so he gave her the name Fluffie. Bob ran a tire dealership and thought having a baby elephant would be a great gimmick to attract customers. It worked like a charm.

Even though Fluffie was small, at just under a metre tall (3 feet) and 371 kilograms (700 pounds) in weight, people flocked to see her. Many visitors had never seen a live elephant before.

At the tire dealership, Fluffie lived in the back of a delivery truck. Bob drove her home with him at night. At first, Fluffie found everything unusual and frightening, but she became more at ease with each passing day.

Carol Buckley, a first-year student in an exotic-animal course at a local college, lived close to the tire dealership. One day, she saw Bob walking Fluffie down the street. Soon, Carol was showing up at the store to offer her services as a volunteer elephant keeper. Bob accepted Carol's offer. It wasn't long before Carol was spending all her free time with Fluffie.

In the 1970s, Tarra appeared in an episode of the popular TV series *Little House on the Prairie.*

Like most baby elephants, Fluffie wanted companionship, comfort and fun; she loved to play. Fluffie was soon going back to Carol's house at night. She'd play in the backyard and she even made a friend: Carol's dog, Tasha. Eventually, Fluffie was only going to the tire dealership on weekends.

Carol quickly realized that Fluffie was smart: she was adept at learning tricks and began performing at parties and fairs and on television shows. After her second birthday, Fluffie became a performer at a theme park and Carol changed her name to Tarra.

While Carol acted as Tarra's caretaker, she was working to convince Bob to sell Tarra to her. Eventually, Bob agreed to the request and Carol became Tarra's official guardian. Carol and Tarra continued to perform at the theme park for the next two years. Then, Carol decided they should perform on the road.

At 6 years old, Tarra stood more than 1.5 metres (5 feet) tall and weighed approximately 1.8 tonnes (2 tons). She performed tricks well, so Carol had special roller skates made and taught Tarra how to use them. By the early 1980s, Tarra was one of the most famous elephants in the world. She performed in circuses and shows across North America and even walked across the stage to present

Tarra became famous as the only roller-skating elephant in the world.

a winning envelope at the 1985 Academy Awards. Those times were full of experiences that were strange and fascinating to Tarra. It was an unusual life for an elephant, but with Carol at her side every step of the way, it was interesting and safe.

As Tarra grew older, though, she seemed to be getting bored with the tricks. So, for five years, Tarra spent the summer seasons giving rides at zoos, performing in TV commercials and making special appearances at various events. When they weren't out working, Carol and Tarra lived in Ojai, California, on a piece of land in a national forest where they could walk through the natural terrain every day.

Carol got a job looking after elephants at a Canadian zoo, so she and Tarra headed north. Some other elephants at the zoo didn't get along with Tarra, though, so Carol and Tarra headed off to the

Racine Zoo in Wisconsin. There, Tarra met the zoo's lone Asian elephant, Rasha, and the two became friends.

Since Tarra and Rasha were both of breeding age, they were taken back up to Canada in 1991, this time to the African Lion Safari where there were bull elephants. The staff hoped they would breed and produce calves of their own.

Tarra didn't bond with the other elephants and seemed to prefer hanging out with only Rasha. Less than two years later, Rasha was sent back to Wisconsin, leaving Tarra alone with the bull elephants. Not long after Rasha left, Tarra became pregnant, but after 22 months, her calf was **stillborn**. It was a distressing time for Tarra. No elephant mother wants to lose her baby.

Scott Blais, a keeper at the safari, became close to Tarra. He and Carol both looked after Tarra and stayed with her after the stillbirth. They provided a great deal of comfort to Tarra and got her through that tough period in her life.

With the passing time, Carol started to worry about Tarra's future. She knew Tarra no longer liked performing, and she didn't want Tarra to stand around in a small zoo enclosure for the rest of her life.

Carol decided to start an elephant sanctuary and Scott Blais agreed to help. They found a property in Tennessee that had lots of natural terrain. At 45 hectares (112 acres), it would be larger than any zoo enclosure. Carol sold her property in California and used the money to help fund the new sanctuary. Tarra would be the sanctuary's first resident.

When Tarra arrived, she quickly made herself at home exploring the fields and forests. She grazed on the grass, pulled at the trees, and bathed in the ponds. Soon, Tarra was no longer alone as other elephants in need began to arrive at the sanctuary.

When other elephants arrived, Tarra would lead them through the barn and the forest. While she developed close relationships with the other elephants who came to the sanctuary, she didn't have a best friend until she met Bella.

Bella was one of the stray dogs that also found a home at the sanctuary. It's possible that Tarra's long-ago friendship with Carol's

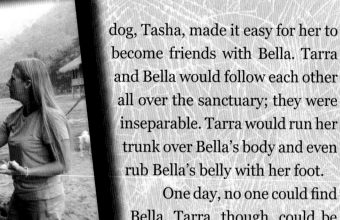

dog, Tasha, made it easy for her to become friends with Bella. Tarra and Bella would follow each other all over the sanctuary; they were inseparable. Tarra would run her trunk over Bella's body and even rub Bella's belly with her foot.

One day, no one could find Bella. Tarra, though, could be found standing in one specific area. When staff members conducted a search, they found Bella lying in a ditch, unable to move. She was taken to a veterinarian who discovered that she had suffered a spinal injury. Bella was brought back to the sanctuary office, next to the elephant barn, for rest and recovery. For two days, Tarra waited patiently at the area where Bella was found. Then, she walked to the elephant barn, where she could see Bella through the windows. Because Tarra was clearly worried for her best friend, the staff carried Bella down to visit her at the barn. They were both overjoyed to be reunited. Tarra returned to the barn every day to see Bella.

The story of Tarra and Bella warmed the hearts of people around the world. Photos of them walking and playing together were seen by millions of people. They remained great friends until Bella passed away in 2011.

The Elephant Sanctuary grew to be 1,092 hectares (2,700 acres) in size, making it the largest natural-habitat elephant facility in the world. In 2009, Carol left the sanctuary and started Elephant Aid International to help other elephants around the world. Tarra still lives happily at The Elephant Sanctuary.

Elephant Aid International promotes compassionate elephant care around the world.

A Carol Buckley Project • www.ElephantAid.org

ELEPHANT AID INTERNATIONAL
One World...One Elephant at a Time

With proper resources and support, park rangers and law enforcement personnel can fight elephant poaching.

ELEPHANT FUTURES

CHAPTER 12

ENSURING WILD ELEPHANTS SURVIVE

If wild elephants are to survive into the future, humans must take several key steps to protect them.

1. Elephants need to be protected from illegal poaching in the parks, reserves and natural areas where they live. Law-enforcement agencies and governments must put money and resources into protecting elephants. Park rangers need more support, and tough laws must be passed, with long jail sentences for poachers.

2. The international trade in elephant ivory must be banned. Individual countries should also ban the trade and sale of ivory within their borders. If there is no trade, elephants will not be killed.

3 Governments in ivory-consuming nations must take steps to educate their citizens about how the ivory trade is destroying elephant populations and convince them to never buy ivory products.

4 Wild elephant habitats need to be protected. Elephants need large areas to live in. In many areas, elephant habitats are decreasing in size as land is taken for human use. In other areas, particularly in India and other parts of southern Asia, elephant habitats are already small and fragmented, and elephants must travel beyond their boundaries to obtain enough food to survive. That leads to human-elephant conflict situations that can result in both human and elephant fatalities.

Elephants have inhabited wild spaces for millions of years, but their future is not secure. We now have a choice to make. We can take steps to ensure they survive, or we can let them fade away until the only elephants we see are in photos and movies.

If no one purchased ivory products, then elephants would not be killed.

GOOD NEWS FOR ELEPHANTS
TECHNOLOGY HELPING ELEPHANTS

Governments are already using technology to help save elephants. In South Sudan, wild elephants have been fitted with GPS collars so their movements can be tracked remotely by satellite. Knowing exactly where the elephants go means they can be better protected. The program is part of a larger project that also includes aerial surveillance and anti-poaching patrols.

In 2013, a team of researchers in the United States announced that they had figured out a way to determine when an elephant's tusks were grown and when the elephant who produced the tusks had died. Being able to date a tusk is an effective tool in fighting the ivory trade. It will reveal if the tusk was acquired before the 1989 African ivory-trade ban, or if it was obtained illegally after that date.

CHANGING THE CAPTIVITY OF ELEPHANTS

Many long-term studies of wild elephants clearly show which physical and social conditions elephants require in order to thrive. Unfortunately, many elephants in captivity are still kept in poor conditions, where they lack space, exercise, freedom of choice, family groups and suitable climate. A few zoos are working hard to improve the lives of elephants, but for many zoos, it is just business as usual.

Many people now suggest that elephant keeping in city zoos should be phased out. Until a phase-out happens, however, zoos have to do everything possible to substantially improve the lives and welfare of the elephants they keep captive.

MUST WE KEEP ELEPHANTS?

In recent years, a number of progressive zoos have decided to end their elephant-keeping because they realized they couldn't provide elephants with enough space or proper care. Others simply decided that feeding and housing elephants is too costly.

In 2001, the UK's London Zoo closed its 170-year-old elephant exhibit and relocated its three female Asian elephants, Mya, Layang-Layang and Dilberta, to Whipsnade Wild Animal Park (now known as the ZSL Whipsnade Zoo). In 2012, officials from the Calgary Zoo in Canada announced their decision to stop keeping elephants and to move their existing herd to another facility. In 2013, they sent their bull elephant to a US zoo and their three female elephants will be moved in 2014. In October 2013, the City of Toronto sent their three African elephants to the PAWS sanctuary in California. The list of zoos that have stopped keeping elephants continues to grow each year.

WATCHING ELEPHANTS WITHOUT ELEPHANTS

Imagine being with elephants, experiencing their immense size and astounding features, without having live elephants anywhere near you. That's the idea behind the Elephant Labyrinth, a unique concept developed by Toronto's ARK architecture company for the animal-welfare organization Zoocheck. Once the Elephant Labyrinth is

The Elephant Labyrinth is a concept that shows that you can learn about elephants without having them in zoos.

built, you will be able to stand in a special theatre where you're entirely surrounded by giant screens showing wild elephants grazing on the African savanna. You'll hear their trumpets and the sounds of their footsteps. You'll feel the pulse of their low rumbles passing through your body. You'll be able to compare your height to the height of an adult bull or compare the weight of your whole family to a baby elephant. The possibilities are endless. The Elephant Labyrinth hasn't been built yet, but when it is, it will show the world that people can learn and experience elephants without keeping them in captivity.

SANCTUARIES AND SAFE HAVENS

In several areas around the world, dedicated animal lovers have created elephant sanctuaries that provide permanent homes to elephants in need. They have also built rescue centres that seek to help elephants on a temporary basis. The sanctuaries and rescue centres often provide more space than zoos, as well as enhanced environments. They allow elephants to choose their own partners and friends, and they are located in elephant-friendly climates.

Sanctuaries and rescue centres do not chain elephants by their legs; they do not strike them with bullhooks or other implements; they do not confine them for long periods indoors; they do not force them to perform tricks; and they do not breed elephants. The people who run these facilities want their elephants to live as similarly as possible to their wild relatives. If the elephants are able to live normally, they have a good chance of improving their health, welfare and quality of life, even if they arrive with serious health problems.

Space and natural conditions make life more interesting at the Elephant Nature Park.

Elephant sanctuaries and rescue centres provide larger spaces and more enhanced conditions than most zoos.

ELEPHANT NATURE PARK

In a natural valley surrounded by forested mountains, the Elephant Nature Park (ENP) provides sanctuary for abused and unwanted elephants from all over Thailand. At 800 hectares (2,000 acres), it provides lots of space for elephants to move and act naturally. Founded in 1996 by Sangduen "Lek" Chailert and her husband, the ENP has taken in 37 elephants, including some that were orphaned, blind or disabled.

Recognizing that many other elephants throughout Thailand also need assistance, the ENP operates a program to provide care to elephants in remote regions of the country. While there are other elephant facilities in Thailand, the ENP is the only one that serves as a rescue centre and sanctuary.

Providing a proper milk substitute and constant companionship is vital to the health and wellbeing of orphaned elephant calves.

DAVID SHELDRICK WILDLIFE TRUST

The David Sheldrick Wildlife Trust, a leader in the rehabilitation and reintroduction to the wild of orphaned elephant calves, can be found just outside the city of Nairobi, Kenya. So far, more than 80 infant elephants have been raised and released back into the wild. At first, keeping the babies healthy was a challenge, but over the years, Trust workers have figured out the best way to feed and raise baby elephants. Knowing that elephant calves depend on their mothers' nutrient-filled milk for approximately two years in the wild, Trust workers knew they needed something just as good. It was difficult, but they eventually developed the first wholesome elephant-milk substitute. With the milk substitute, orphaned elephant calves can survive at the centre until they are old enough to be released back into the wild.

The Trust also operates a mobile veterinary clinic, runs community education programs, and sends out patrols to remove traps that illegally capture wild animals.

PERFORMING ANIMAL WELFARE SOCIETY'S ARK 2000 SANCTUARY

Founded by former Hollywood Animal Trainer Pat Derby and her partner Ed Stewart, the Performing Animal Welfare Society's ARK 2000 sanctuary in San Andreas, California, is an elephant paradise. The sanctuary's massive enclosures provide a variety of terrain for elephants to walk or forage, bathe in the mud, interact with companions or just

The PAWS sanctuary recently became the new home of Toronto elephant Thika and her companions Toka and Iringa.

get away on their own. The space and complexity of the sanctuary ensure that the elephants are stimulated and never get bored. This sanctuary leads by example and shows that when elephants are kept in captivity, there's a humane way to do it.

NEW ELEPHANT SANCTUARIES

With so many elephants in need, it's no surprise that new elephant sanctuaries are being planned and built. The Indian animal-protection organization Wildlife SOS has recently set up Elephant Haven, which is already populated by several retired elephants. Wildlife SOS is also currently working with the Haryana Forest Department to establish the Elephant Rehabilitation and Research Centre, a facility that will provide sanctuary for abused, ill, injured or old elephants. Another Elephant Haven, a 50-hectare (123 acre) European elephant sanctuary, has been proposed. With multiple heated barns, **quarantine facilities** and enough space for elephants to roam and graze, the sanctuary will provide an alternative for European elephants in need. Scott Blais, co-founder of The Elephant Sanctuary in Tennessee, where Tarra lives, is now working to establish an elephant sanctuary in Brazil.

Game reserves provide expansive natural environments for elephants and other animals.

CHAIN-FREE CORRALS

With so many Asian street elephants on chains, Elephant Aid International began a project to provide an alternative—the Chain-Free Corral. Using solar-powered electric fences with battery backups, both forested and open areas are enclosed. This allows street elephants to be chain-free, so they can move around in large areas and engage in natural behaviours, like browsing, dusting and walking. The **corrals** eliminate the stress of chains and increase elephant welfare.

While animals in game reserves are wild, they may become used to the reserve staff who monitor and protect them.

REWILDING—GAME RESERVES

Throughout Africa, there are hundreds of private game reserves where animals roam in a wild state. While many of these reserves are fenced, the animals that live in them can sometimes travel for hours or days without ever seeing a fence. In reserves that keep elephants, the animals find their own food, shelter and companions.

Game reserves not only protect high-profile animals, like elephants and rhinos, but they also safeguard the environment and all of the other animals and plants that live there, too. A single reserve may have just one type of habitat or a variety of terrain, including grasslands, forests, river valleys and marshes.

Game reserves may be suitable homes for many animals that have spent their lives in captivity. While there are risks in moving an elephant or any other animal from captivity to a wild environment, past attempts have proven that many animals will not only survive, they'll thrive. The term that is often used to describe preparing a long-term captive animal for release is **rewilding**. Rewilding can be a humane option for many captive animals.

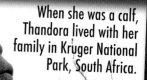
When she was a calf, Thandora lived with her family in Kruger National Park, South Africa.

FIVE ELEPHANTS
THANDORA'S LEGACY

Thandora was just 4 or 5 years old when her family was killed during a **culling** operation in South Africa's Kruger National Park in 1989. Her life was spared and she was sent off to live in a zoo in Bloemfontein, a small city known for its flowers and annual rose festival.

Culling is a term that means the legal, organized killing of an animal species, like elephants. At the time Kruger National Park managers believed there were too many elephants. They thought the elephants were negatively affecting the park environment and needed to be culled to control their population.

For more than 18 years, Thandora lived at the zoo. At the beginning of her captivity, Thandora shared her enclosure with a bull elephant. When that elephant died, another bull named Marula replaced him. As the years went by, however, Thandora and Marula didn't get along so well. Marula became aggressive and was eventually moved out. For the next 4 years, Thandora lived alone.

As time went by, concern grew about Thandora's living situation. People said her enclosure wasn't adequate—that it was too small and that Thandora didn't have an environment in which she could display normal elephant behaviours. But most of all, she did not have other elephants to socialize with. She was stressed and lonely.

After extensive negotiations between the zoo, groups like Conservation Global, and the local government, it was decided to return Thandora to the wild where she would have the space and conditions she needed to behave in a natural way. She would be moved to the Gondwana Game Reserve. Moving to the wild would also provide Thandora with a chance to meet and socialize with other elephants. The decision to rewild Thandora was based on what was best for her.

The reserve was huge. It consisted of 11,000 hectares (27,181 acres) of grassland, valleys and natural shrubland. Best of all, it was a perfect elephant habitat. Many elephants already resided at Gondwana, including two bulls and two cows that had been successfully rehabilitated onto the reserve.

At the Gondwana Game Reserve, Thandora would gradually transition from zoo food to natural food.

The Thandora Reintroduction Project would be carefully coordinated by the organization Conservation Global and Gondwana Game Reserve staff.

Moving Thandora into a wild home with other elephants wasn't something that could be accomplished overnight. After more than 23 years in the zoo, Thandora's muscles weren't strong. Since the Gondwana elephants often walked 10 to 15 kilometres (6 to 9 miles) each day, Thandora needed to get fit if she was going to keep up.

With all the arrangements in place, Thandora spent 15 hours in a truck being moved to her new home. When she arrived at Gondwana, she was put into a special 1-hectare (2.4 acre) enclosure called a **boma**. On the first day, Thandora was walked for 1 kilometre (0.6 miles) around the boma. She was stiff and she limped a bit.

The plan was for Thandora to stay in the boma for at least 6 to 8 weeks, so she could get used to her new location. She had to build her strength and learn to eat natural vegetation. Hopefully, she would communicate with other elephants outside of the boma as well.

In the boma, Thandora was able to get more exercise and become used to the sights, sounds and smells of a wild environment.

A vehicle provided comfort to Thandora while she became accustomed to her new home.

On the second day, Thandora was walked continuously for 1.5 kilometres (0.9 miles). Wild elephant dung was put into her boma, so she could become more familiar with the scent of the other elephants on the reserve.

When Thandora's caretakers returned on the third day, they discovered she had broken out of the boma and walked almost 3 kilometres (1.8 miles) away. She was found in a thicket and seemed quite content. After a few hours, her caretakers took her back to the boma. They didn't know why she broke out. She might have wanted to join other elephants or she might have been startled by other wild animals. Thandora would

Thandora has paved the way for the rewilding of other elephants in captivity.

be watched 24 hours a day after that break out.

Thandora felt more comfortable with people around, so a vehicle was parked inside the boma. She would often stand next to it as she ate. She seemed to like having it there.

Each day, Thandora was walked a little bit farther, and gradually, she was being shifted over from zoo food to natural food. Thandora found the food harder to manipulate, but she quickly became adept at using her trunk and tusks as feeding aids.

Wild elephants occasionally came to the boma fence. It's likely that Thandora was communicating with them even when they were out of sight. She was gradually becoming more like a wild elephant.

As time passed, Thandora learned to use her environment. She was observed using a large branch to scratch her back, and using the natural vegetation as protection from wind and rain.

On April 22, 2013, Thandora was released from the boma. She was hesitant at first, but she soon made her way out and walked 2 kilometres (1.2 miles) away. Later that first night, she encountered two elephant cows. They all began trumpeting to each other, but when the two cows moved off, Thandora did not follow.

Within the next few days, Thandora met the elephant-cow herd again. They came over and greeted her, but Thandora remained close to the vehicle for comfort. Eventually, the other elephants moved off, but it was clear that Thandora had made new friends.

Another night, Thandora was visited by two bull elephants. Again, she seemed reluctant to join them, and remained close to the vehicle.

On May 23, observers reported that Thandora had joined the bull elephants and had been travelling with them for the previous four days. When it was clear that she was staying with the bulls, the observers left and only returned intermittently to see how she was doing. Each time, Thandora was with the bulls.

For the next week, Thandora behaved like a truly wild elephant. She explored, foraged, grazed, encountered other animals and socialized with other elephants. It was a remarkable transformation.

On June 13, however, Thandora appeared distressed and uncomfortable. She was having trouble standing up. Despite the heroic efforts of the Gondwana Game Reserve caretakers to save her, Thandora passed away that day. Her end came from **botulism**, a rare bacterial illness that usually affects birds and other wildlife.

Although Thandora's death was a freak accident, her astonishing journey has shown that captive elephants can be successfully transitioned to the wild. Thandora is a pioneer who has helped pave the way for others to follow in her footsteps into the wild.

To keep Thandora's legacy alive, Conservation Global created Project Thandora—a project dedicated to ensuring the welfare of elephants in captivity.

Even though Thandora had spent most of her life in captivity, she was rapidly becoming a true wild elephant.

All over the world, people are speaking out for the protection of wild elephants and for an end to the exploitation of elephants in captivity.

CHAPTER 14

HOPE FOR THE FUTURE

There is no doubt that many elephants, both wild and captive, have had tough times. In the wild, elephants like Echo and her family deal with all of the natural challenges that elephants face, such as drought and lack of food. They've evolved to deal with these types of challenges and have been highly successful. But the challenges created by humans, like ivory poaching, habitat destruction and human-elephant conflicts, are much more difficult and dangerous.

In captivity, elephants like Tusko and Lucy must deal with a whole different set of challenges. These issues can include lack of space, not enough stimulation and exercise, unnatural social groups, disease, poor health and psychological problems.

Luckily, things are starting to change. People all over the world are concerned about elephants and want to help. They want wild elephants to be protected and captive elephants to be treated better.

The unique relationship between Tarra and Carol Buckley led to the creation of The Elephant Sanctuary and an entirely different way of keeping elephants in captivity. Thandora's journey has taught us that returning to the wild is possible for some captive elephants.

The tireless efforts of people, young and old, to help stop the ivory trade and to protect wild elephant habitats can lead to a bright future for elephants. The many new elephant sanctuaries and rescue centres, along with changes in traditional elephant captivity in zoos, and new ideas, like the Elephant Labyrinth, provide hope for elephants everywhere.

Far too many elephants are still kept in poor conditions in zoos. It is time for zoos to recognize they can't provide the conditions elephants need.

While I was writing this book, United States President Barack Obama announced the creation of an Advisory Council on Wildlife Trafficking and the US destroyed its ivory stockpile. The Clinton Global Initiative announced an $80 million effort to save African elephants, and the co-founder of Microsoft computers, Paul Allen, said he would fund a survey to determine exactly how many elephants are left in the wild. China also announced that it would take steps to deal with ivory smuggling. That is good progress for wild elephants.

I hope the information and stories in this book encourage you to become an Elephant Guardian. Things are changing, but elephants still need help. They need you to become an Elephant Guardian, too.

HOW TO BECOME AN ELEPHANT GUARDIAN

1. Do not buy carvings or other products made from ivory. If no one purchased ivory, elephants would not be killed for their tusks.

2. Inform your family, friends and classmates about elephant issues in captivity (such as small spaces, the ankus and elephant chaining) and in the wild (such as poaching and habitat loss).

3. Do not attend circuses or shows that feature elephant performances or elephant rides.

4. Investigate whether your local zoo keeps elephants and what their conditions are like. If you don't like what you find, let people know about your concerns, and advocate for the elephants to be moved to better conditions.

5. Speak up for elephants. Start a letter-writing campaign to voice your concerns about the treatment of elephants in captivity or in the wild. Send your letters to newspapers, government officials, animal-protection groups and zoos.

There are stickers and information available from many elephant protection groups. Contact them to find out how they can help you spread the word.

Start a campaign in your school to raise funds to adopt an elephant at an elephant sanctuary or rescue centre or to support an elephant-protection project in the wild.

 Create a website, blog or Facebook page about elephant welfare and protection issues.

 Support animal-welfare groups that work to improve the lives of elephants in captivity and organizations that work to protect elephants in the wild. Look up elephant campaigns on the internet to find both wild and captive elephant campaigns that you can help support.

⑨ Raise funds or help publicize elephant sanctuaries that provide permanent homes for abused, unwanted or retired captive elephants, or rescue centres that take in orphaned or injured elephants for rehabilitation and release back to the wild.

ELEPHANT-WELFARE ORGANIZATIONS

Amboseli Trust for Elephants
www.elephanttrust.org

Animal Defenders International
www.ad-international.org

Born Free Foundation
www.bornfree.org.uk

Conservation Global
www.conservationglobal.org

Eco-Sys Action
www.ecosysaction.org

Elephant Aid International
www.elephantaidinternational.org

Elephant Haven
www.elephanthaven.com

Elephant Nature Park
www.elephantnaturepark.org

Elephant Neighbors Center
www.elephantneighborscenter.org

Elephant Voices
www.elephantvoices.org

Elephants Without Borders
www.elephantswithoutborders.org

Global Sanctuary for Elephants
www.sanctuaryforelephants.org

International Fund for Animal Welfare
www.ifaw.org

In Defense of Animals
www.idausa.org

Performing Animal Welfare Society (PAWS)
www.pawsweb.org

Save the Elephants
www.savetheelephants.org

The David Sheldrick Wildlife Trust
www.sheldrickwildlifetrust.org

The Elephant Sanctuary
www.elephants.com

Voice for Animals Humane Society
www.v4a.org

Wildlife SOS
www.wildlifesos.org

Zoocheck
www.zoocheck.com

GLOSSARY

Allomother: a female elephant who comforts, assists and protects the calves of other female elephants

Ankus: a short stick with a sharp point and a curved metal hook that is used to control and guide elephants

Black market: the illegal trade of a product, such as elephant ivory

Boma: a livestock enclosure, often used to contain large mammals

Bond group: two or more related elephant family groups that associate with one another

Botulism: a disease caused by a toxin

Breeding loan: the transfer of animals from one zoo to another for breeding purposes

Bull elephant: an adult male elephant

Calves: two or more infant or young elephants

Clan: a large group of elephants made up of several bond groups and families

Conservation: the protection of animals, plants and natural areas

Conservationists: people who work to protect and conserve wild animals and the habitats in which they live

Convention on International Trade in Endangered Species: an international treaty (law) to control the trade of endangered animals and plants

Corral: a fenced pen or enclosure

Cow elephant: an adult female elephant

Culling: the legal killing of animals for population control purposes

Dentine: the hard, bony material that teeth and tusks are made of

Digital pad: large pads of fat in the foot that act as cushions while walking

Ecology: a branch of science that looks at living things and their relationships to the environments in which they live

Elephant calf: an infant or young elephant

Enrichment: adding furnishings, objects or activities, or making other changes to keep animals in captivity occupied

Extinction: the state when all members of a species have died out

Fertility: the ability to breed and produce young

Fragmented: broken up into pieces

Herbivores: animals that feed on grass and other plants

Hobbles: chains or tethers that bind two or more legs

Incisor teeth: in elephants, cheek teeth that grow to become tushes or tusks

Infrasound: low sounds that can travel long distances, which humans often can't hear

Ivory: the material that elephant tusks are made of

Ivory trade: the commercial, and often illegal, selling of ivory tusks

Keystone species: an animal or plant that plays a major role in the functioning of the ecosystem in which it lives

Lifespan: the amount of time that an animal lives

Mahout: an Indian word for a person who owns and rides an elephant

Matriarch: a mature female elephant who acts as a leader of a family

Militia: a group whose members are trained as soldiers but are not part of a country's military forces

Musth: a periodic condition experienced by adult bull elephants in which there is a substantial rise in reproductive hormones

Pachyderm: an old term for a large animal with hooves and thick skin, like an elephant or hippopotamus

Poaching: the illegal hunting, killing or collection of wild animals or plants

Proboscis: the elephant trunk

Quarantine facilities: areas where elephants are temporarily separated to check for or prevent the spread of disease

Rewilding: the process of preparing an animal to live in the wild

Smuggling: the hidden, usually illegal, transport of an item, like elephant ivory

Stereotypies: meaningless, repetitive movements, like rocking or pacing, which don't occur in wild animals

Stillborn: when a baby is not alive when born

Timber operations: cutting down and removing trees for wood while using elephants for labour

Tushes: small tusks that often don't protrude past an elephant's lip

"In this, his latest in a wonderful series of children's books, author and animal protectionist Rob Laidlaw helps us understand the issues and challenges faced by both captive and wild elephants. He explores the challenges that elephants face, by focusing on one famous elephant at a time, all five giving us a broad sense of the negative and positive sides of our relations and dealings with these complex, social and ecologically important animals."

BARRY KENT MACKAY, CANADIAN REPRESENTATIVE OF BORN FREE USA, NATURALIST-ARTIST, AUTHOR

"Rob Laidlaw is one of Canada's foremost experts on zoos and wildlife issues. Impassioned, informative and interesting, his book *5 Elephants* is a wonderful resource for young readers who care about animals. It is an intelligent and reliable guide to very serious issues but sends an empowering message to young people that they can change the world for the better."

DR. JOHN SORENSON, AUTHOR, PROFESSOR, BROCK UNIVERSITY

"This is the best kid's book about these most amazing and majestic animals of which I am aware. Indeed, it's much more than that, because anyone who wants to learn about the fascinating lives of elephants—their ups and downs and twists and turns—will walk away with a wealth of knowledge. [. . .] I learned a lot from reading it and plan to share it widely."

MARC BEKOFF, AUTHOR OF *THE EMOTIONAL LIVES OF ANIMALS*, *JASPER'S STORY: SAVING MOON BEARS* (WITH JILL ROBINSON), AND EDITOR OF *IGNORING NATURE NO MORE: THE CASE FOR COMPASSIONATE CONSERVATION*

"For anyone, child or adult, who loves elephants (and who doesn't?) and is concerned about the survival of the species, this is an informative and compelling read."

TOVE REECE, VOICE FOR ANIMALS HUMANE SOCIETY (EDMONTON)

"In *5 Elephants*, Rob Laidlaw brings to life not just the dignity and intelligence of these charismatic animals, but how they suffer at the hands of humans. He paints a vivid portrait of five elephants who have had a powerful impact on society and explores the role that poaching and habitat loss have played in fragmenting populations that once ranged across most of Africa and Asia. [. . .] Filled with fascinating facts—who knew an elephant's trunk contains 60,000 muscles?—*5 Elephants* is certain to thrill and educate animal lovers of all ages."

MARK HAWTHORNE, AUTHOR OF *BLEATING HEARTS: THE HIDDEN WORLD OF ANIMAL SUFFERING*

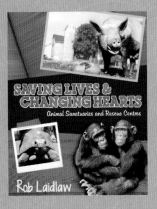

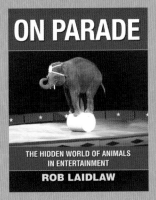

PRAISE FOR
SAVING LIVES AND CHANGING HEARTS: ANIMAL SANCTUARIES AND RESCUE CENTRES

Nominated for the Ontario Library Association Silver Birch Award for Non-Fiction Shortlisted for the 2014 Rocky Mountain Book Award Nominated in the Favourite Book of the Year category for the Vegetarian Association's 2013 Toronto Veg Awards

"*Saving Lives and Changing Hearts: Animal Sanctuaries and Rescue Centres* sends an important message of compassion and hope in a world full of unthinkable cruelty. It should be in every school and public library."

PETE AND SIOBHAN POOLE, FOUNDERS, THE CEDAR ROW FARM SANCTUARY

"Simple, compelling, complete. *Saving Lives and Changing Hearts: Animal Sanctuaries and Rescue Centres* is a moving look at the important role of sanctuaries to individual animals, animal welfare and conservation!"

BARB CARTWRIGHT, CEO, CANADIAN FEDERATION OF HUMANE SOCIETIES

PRAISE FOR
ON PARADE: THE HIDDEN WORLD OF ANIMALS IN ENTERTAINMENT

Winner of the Vancouver Children's Literature Roundtable Information Book Award Winner of a Skipping Stones Honor Award

"After working many years with Nancy Burnet, of United Activists for Animal Rights, exposing cruelty to animals in entertainment, I can assure you that such cruelty is rampant. Rob Laidlaw's book, *On Parade*, tells the tragic story of animal suffering for man's diversion in vivid, heartbreaking detail. Read it, and help us save these pitiful creatures from the clutches of those who would do them harm."

BOB BARKER, TELEVISION PERSONALITY AND ACTIVIST

"Wonderful, solid, educational and absorbing. This book gives every young reader a lesson in our evolving idea of who animals are and our obligations to respect them."

INGRID NEWKIRK, PRESIDENT, PEOPLE FOR THE ETHICAL TREATMENT OF ANIMALS

PRAISE FOR
WILD ANIMALS IN CAPTIVITY

Nominated for the Ontario Library Association Silver Birch Award for Non-Fiction

"Rob Laidlaw has been working tirelessly on behalf of animals in zoos ever since I met him many years ago. This well-written book, with its carefully chosen examples and photographs, is a fair assessment of what is bad, better, and best for animals in this world of captivity. It will help you to judge for yourself whether or not the conditions are suitable so that, when necessary, you can speak out on behalf of some unhappy animal prisoner."

DR. JANE GOODALL, FOUNDER, JANE GOODALL INSTITUTE, UN MESSENGER OF PEACE

"[This] is a great book that not only explains the problems of keeping wild animals in captivity in an easy to understand and entertaining way, it also provides ways for the reader to make a difference and help the animals themselves."

DAVE EASTHAM, HEAD OF WILDLIFE, WORLD SOCIETY FOR THE PROTECTION OF ANIMALS

BIBLIOGRAPHY

Buckley, Carol, *Travels with Tarra*, Tilbury House Publishers, Gardiner, ME, USA, 2002

Forthman, Debra, Kane, Lisa. F., Hancocks, David and Paul F. Waldau (eds.), *An Elephant in the Room: The Science and Well-Being of Elephants in Captivity*, Tufts Center for Animals and Public Policy, North Grafton, MA, USA, 2009

Ghosh, Rhea, *Gods in Chains*, Foundation Books, New Delhi, India 2005

Jordan, Dr. W. J., Poole, Dr. J., Sheldrick, D. and L. Gillson, *Elephants,* Care for the Wild International, West Sussex, UK, 1998

Lavigne, David (ed.), *Elephants & Ivory*, International Fund for Animals Welfare, Yarmouth Port, MA, USA, 2013

Lewis, George and Byron Fish, *I Loved Rogues*, Superior Publishing Company, Seattle, WA USA, 1978

Moss, Cynthia, Crose, Harvey and Phyllis C. Lee (eds.), *The Amboseli Elephants, A Long-Term Perspective On A Long-Lived Mammal*, University of Chicago Press, Chicago, IL, USA, 2011

Moss, Cynthia, *Elephant Memories, Thirteen Years in the Life of an Elephant Family*, University of Chicago Press, Chicago, IL, USA, 2000

Orenstein, Ronald (ed.), *Elephants, The Deciding Decade*, Key Porter Books, Toronto, Canada, 1991

Orenstein, Ronald, *Ivory, Horn and Blood, Behind the Elephant and Rhinocerous Poaching Crisis*, Firefly Books, Richmond Hill, Canada, 2013

Redmond, Ian, *Elephant*, Stoddart Publishing Co., Toronto, Canada, 1993

Redmond, Ian, *The Elephant in the Bush*, Gareth Stevens Children's Book, Milwaukee, WI, USA, 1990

Schmidt, Michael, *Jumbo Ghosts, The Dangerous Life Of Elephants In The Zoo*, Xlibris Corp., Bloomington, IN, USA, 2001

Shoshani, Jeheskel (ed.), *Elephants, Majestic Creatures of the Wild*, Rodale Press Inc., Emmaus, PA, USA, 1992

Sukumar, Raman, *The Living Elephants, Evolutionary Ecology, Behaviour and Conservation*, Oxford University Press, New York, USA, 2003

Wemmer, Christen and Catherine A. Christen, *Elephants and Ethics, Toward A Morality of Coexistence*, The John Hopkins University Press, Baltimore, MA, USA, 2008

Wylie, Dan, *Elephant*, Reaktion Books, London, UK, 2008

INDEX

IMAGE CREDITS